THE TABLETOP LEARNING SERIES

GAMES

Some Old, Some New, All Fun To Do

by Imogene Forte

Incentive Publications, Inc.
Nashville, Tennessee

Illustrated by Mary Hamilton
Cover designed by Mary Hamilton and illustrated by Jan Cunningham
Edited by Susan Oglander

Library of Congress Catalog Number 83-82331
ISBN 0-86530-093-3

THIS
GAMES BOOK
BELONGS TO

_____

CONTENTS

PEACE AND QUIET

A NOTE TO KIDS

At last,here's a book that offers all kinds of games for all kinds of occasions and all kinds of kids. If you feel like making some noise, there are noisy games, or if you want some quiet time, there are games to play alone—plus, word games, contests, guessing games, and games for traveling and rainy days. Many of the games are old favorites that your parents may have played, some are brand new, and some are old-fashioned but with a new twist. There are some that will start your head spinning, some to tease your brain, and others to help you relax and let off steam. All the game rules are simple and easy to follow, and none require much material or equipment.

Be sure to add your own games on the pages provided for that purpose. Then your Games Book will become your very own personal reference for fun and learning experiences. The amusing animal illustrations will surely set the mood for the excitement you will have with this little book.

Imogene Forte

WHO WILL BE "IT"?

Sometimes, determining who will be "it" becomes a fun game in itself. Many games call for a leader or a player to be "it." Here are some ways to select the first "it" to get your game going.

- Ask someone not in the game to write a number on a piece of paper. Then, all the players try to guess the number. The player whose guess is the closest is "it."

- Tear strips of paper into different lengths and put them in a bowl or jar. The player who draws the shortest strip is "it." If you are playing outside, sticks may be used instead of paper.

- Place kernels of corn in a cup or box—all white or red, except for one of the opposite color. Each player draws a kernel of corn, and the player who draws the odd color is "it." Pieces of colored paper or red and black checkers can be substituted for the corn.

- One player bounces a ball twice, then throws it out chanting, "bouncing ball, bouncing ball, I'm out." The other players scramble to get the ball. The one who gets it repeats the chant, bounces the ball twice, and throws it again. This continues until only one player is left to become "it."

- One person calls out a number larger than the number of players and says, "_____ number out." Then, he counts around the group until he reaches the player that the number falls on, and that player becomes "it."

- Each player picks up a small stone and the person with the largest stone is "it."

- One player tosses a coin, covers it with his hand, and asks another player to guess "heads" or "tails." The loser tosses the coin again and asks another player to call "heads" or "tails." The game continues until the last loser becomes "it."

- All players sit in a circle. One person calls out the letters of the alphabet, touching each player as he moves around the circle. When he touches a person whose last name begins with the letter called, that person is out. The game continues in this way until only one player is left to become "it."

- All players sit in a circle while someone chants,

  Eenie, meenie, minie, mo,
  Catch a tiger by the toe,
  If he hollers make him pay,
  Fifty dollars every day,
  My mother told me
  To pick the very best one
  And that is you!

  while pointing to a player as each word is called. The person on whom "you" falls is out. The game continues until only one player is left to become "it."

- Some other rhymes you can use in the same way are:

  Two, four, six, eight
  You're the one we appreciate!

  One, two, three,
  Bobby caught a flea,
  The flea flew away,
  One, two, three.

  One, two, three, four, five, six, seven,
  Pick up three, add one and you have eleven.

For fun, try making up some counting rhymes of your own.

ON YOUR MARK, GET SET, GO!

games and contests to get things moving

MY OWN IDEAS

PICK-A-MOVE
and remember the others too!

Players form a circle. If there are only two players, they stand facing each other. One player starts the game by making a movement of some sort, like jogging in place, snapping fingers, hopping on one foot, or clapping. The next player repeats the movement and adds one of his own. Each player in turn adds a new movement after repeating the previous ones. Players are out of the game when they forget a movement or repeat it in the wrong order. The last one left is the winner. Pick-a-Move is fun for the players and for onlookers too!

tap!

PAY THE PENALTY

a great icebreaker

A Judge and a Jury Foreman are selected. The other players sit in a row and each one gives some small personal item (a comb, bracelet, cap) to the Jury Foreman. The items are placed in a box or basket. The Judge sits facing the players with his back to the Jury Foreman. The Jury Foreman selects an item and holds it over the Judge's head saying, "Heavy, heavy hangs over your head. What penalty shall the owner pay?" Without seeing the item or knowing who it belongs to, the Judge names a penalty the owner must pay to get the item back.

The fun of this game depends on how creative the Judge can be in thinking up silly things for the players to do. For example, sing a silly song all the way through without stopping, spell the full name of the school principal, take ten steps backward with your eyes closed and your hands at your side, repeat the alphabet backward, or give a one minute talk on penguins!

TOSS UP
the end of the month scores more

For this game you will need a page from a calendar that has fairly large blocks for each day of the month, and some small rocks.

Each player tosses a rock onto the calendar. The date that the rock lands on is the number of points the player receives. If the rock lands between two dates, the lower number is added to the score. The player with the highest score after three tosses is the winner.

BALLOON ROUNDUP
elbows, heads, and feet work well

For this game you will need balloons and large containers (baskets or boxes).

Blow up several balloons of equal shape and size. (Round balloons are the most fun for this game.) Toss the balloons in the air. The object of the game is for players to get balloons into a basket or box without using their hands. The player who gets the most balloons into her container wins the game.

To make the game more interesting, try these variations.
- Mark the balloons with the numbers one through ten. The winner is the player or team scoring the most points.
- Use colors or numbers to designate balloons for individual players or teams. (Only one container is needed for this variation.) For example, Player A can only count red and green balloons. Player B can only count yellow and blue balloons. Team number one can only count balloons marked #1. Team number two can only count balloons marked #2. If team number one puts a #2 balloon in the box, team number two gets the point!

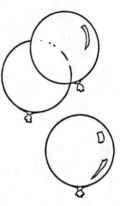

LONG DISTANCE CALLING

a chance to let off steam

One person is selected to be the Telephone Operator, and another the Supervisor. All the other players select the name of a city or country.

The Supervisor goes around to each player and makes a list of all the cities and countries, and uses it to "call from." All the players are seated in chairs placed in a circle except the Telephone Operator and the Supervisor. The Telephone Operator and the Supervisor stand in the center of the circle.

The Supervisor says, "Ring! Ring! London calling Paris" (or any other two cities or countries from the list). The players whose cities or countries are named, must run to exchange places before the Telephone Operator can catch one of them. They cannot be caught after they have changed places. Once a player is caught, he or she becomes the Telephone Operator. If the Supervisor fails to say "Ring! Ring!" before naming the two cities or countries, he or she must change places with the Telephone Operator.

To make the the game livelier, the Supervisor may occasionally call "Ring! Ring! Lines crossed, telephone scramble" and all players including the Telephone Operator must change chairs. The player left with no chair becomes the next Telephone Operator.

Players should take turns being the Supervisor.

STOP THE MUSIC
and grab a chair!

For this game you will need a piano or record player, someone to start and "stop the music," and chairs for all but one of the players.

The chairs should be placed back to back in a row. The players line up and when the music begins, they skip around the chairs. When the music suddenly stops, each player rushes to get a chair. The player left standing is out of the game. One chair is removed each time before the music begins again, and the game continues until only one player is left to become the winner.

This is a good game to play when you are tired of being inside on a rainy day or when there's a need to let off a little steam.

TAKE THE PLUNGE
a steady hand is all you need

For this game you will need a plunger, three paper plates, felt tip pens, and scissors.

Cut the centers from three paper plates varying the size of the center circles. The plate with the smallest circle should be colored red, the middle-sized circle should be blue, and the largest circle colored yellow. The red plate is worth 20 points, the blue plate is worth 10 points, and the yellow plate counts 5 points.

Place the plunger in the center of the circle of players. The object of this game is for each player to try to throw the plates onto the plunger handle. Each player gets to toss each plate once, add up the points, and then the next player gets a turn. The player who has the highest score after five turns is the winner.

25

COPY CAT COMMANDS
don't get confused or you'll be out

This is a fun game to play with a group when you need to stretch and relax after a busy time or when you can't get outside to run and play.

One player is selected to be the Copy Cat. The Copy Cat gives orders to the other players such as "Copy Cat commands you to touch your toes," and all the other players must follow the command. If the Copy Cat gives a direction without saying "Copy Cat commands," the player who follows that direction is out of the game. The object of the game is for the Copy Cat to try to confuse the players either by giving directions rapidly, or without saying "Copy Cat commands," or by doing an action different from the command given. For example, the Copy Cat may say, "Copy Cat commands hands on head," and cover his eyes instead.

The player who stays in the game the longest wins and becomes the Copy Cat for the next game.

WORD FINDERS
don't forget to read the fine print

For this game you will need old magazines, scissors, paste, paper, and an alarm clock.

Each player chooses a magazine. A certain word is selected and an amount of time, such as five or ten minutes, in which to find the word is agreed upon. Then, the alarm clock is set for that time period. On the signal "go," players begin looking for the word in their magazines. As players find the word, they cut it out and paste it on their paper. At the end of the allotted time, the player with the most words on the paper wins.

Variation
A number of different words are written on slips of paper, and each player draws a word to find. Discussing the words as players search for them becomes half the fun, especially when players spot an opponent's word. The player with the most words wins.

DREIDEL GAME

to celebrate the Festival of Lights

As part of the Chanukah celebration, Jewish children play the dreidel game. The Hebrew letters on each side of the dreidel stand for "Nes gadol hayah sham," which mean "A great miracle happened there."

Here is how the game goes. Players sit on the floor in a circle. Each player gets some nuts or candies, and the rest are put in the center of the circle or "in the pot." The first player spins the dreidel. If the dreidel lands on "nun," the player doesn't take anything from the pot. If it lands on "gimel," the player takes a handful of nuts. "Shin" means a player must add some of his or her own nuts to the center pot. And if the dreidel lands on "hay," the player must take just a few nuts. The game ends when all the nuts in the center are gone. The player with the most nuts is the winner.

nun   gimel   hay   shin

Use the pattern to make a dreidel of your own. Use blue and white construction paper as these are the traditional Jewish colors. Cut the shape out and fold on the dotted lines to make a cube. Cut out the holes on the top and bottom, and glue the tabs together. After the glue drys, push a short pencil through the holes at the top and bottom and you will have a spinning top!

WHODUNIT??

a wink of the eye is all it takes

For this game you will need slips of paper for each player (only one marked with an X), and a basket or bowl to put them in.

Players sit in a circle within clear view of one another. Each player draws a slip of paper. The one who chooses the paper marked with the X is the Killer. This person begins to exchange glances with everyone and slyly winks at victims without letting anyone else see. The victim waits about three seconds after seeing the wink and says, "I'm dead."

The object of the game is for the Killer to wink at everyone, leaving one person left before being identified. If at anytime during the game, someone thinks he knows who the Killer is, he may announce that person's name. If right, he then becomes the Killer. If wrong, both the accuser and the accused are out of the game and play continues.

TAFFY PULL
a real contest of strength

For this game you will need a large scarf or bandanna.

This game is for two players. Make a line on the floor with chalk or a piece of tape. Each player holds one end of the scarf and sits an equal distance from the line. When someone says "Taffy Pull," both players pull at their ends of the scarf until one player's hand is pulled across the line or one player lets go.

Variation
This game can also be played with teams. But, you must get a scarf (or rope) long enough for each team member to hold on to.

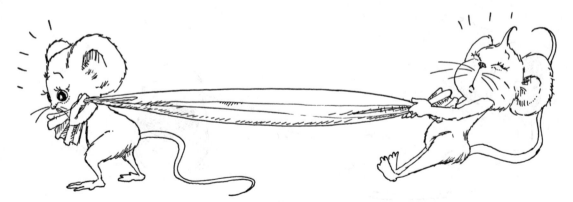

GRAB THE PHONE

and be sure to listen for your name

For this game you will need to make tin can phones. Wash and dry two tin cans. Carefully punch a hole in the bottom of each can with a nail. Thread four to six feet of string through the hole and tie a knot on the inside, joining the two cans. You now have a phone ready to use for the following game. (You can use paper cups instead of cans.)

Approximately ten players are needed for this game divided into teams of five. On each team, someone is selected to be a Caller and a Receiver. The other team members stand a good distance away in a horizontal line. The Caller stands with his back to the team members with one can to his mouth. The

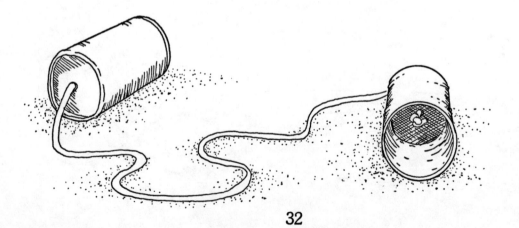

Receiver faces the Caller with the other can to his ear. On the word "go," the Caller says a name of a team member and the Receiver drops the phone and runs to tag that person. The person whose name is called must run and "grab the phone" before the other team does. The Caller then goes back into the line, and the Receiver becomes the Caller. The person whose name was called becomes the Receiver. The team with the most people to "grab the phone" first wins.

THIMBLE, THIMBLE, WHERE'S THE THIMBLE?

if it's found, sit yourself down

This is an old-fashioned game that children and grownups have long enjoyed playing at family get-togethers or on long winter evenings. You may be surprised at how much fun you and your family or friends will have with it.

For this game you will need a thimble. (If you don't have a thimble, a pingpong ball or other small object will do.)

34

One player is selected to hide the thimble. The other players leave the room or close their eyes while the thimble is put in a place where it can be seen, but not easily. The players are then called back into the room or asked to open their eyes, and the search for the thimble begins. As players discover the thimble, they sit down quietly. The first player to spot the thimble and sit down, hides the thimble the next time. The last player to spot the thimble is out of the game. The game continues until only two searchers are left. The first to sit down is declared the winner of the game.

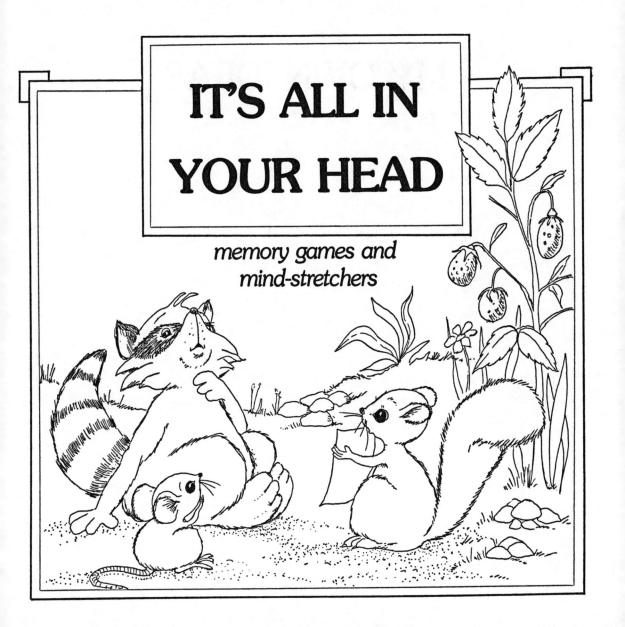

IT'S ALL IN YOUR HEAD

memory games and
mind-stretchers

MY OWN IDEAS

MISSING PERSON
Sherlock Holmes had to start somewhere

This is a game for a large group.

One player is selected to be the Detective. Another player agrees to be the Timekeeper. The other players sit around a table or in a circle on the floor. The Detective turns his back to the group, and one player quietly leaves the room. The other players change places as quickly as possible. The Detective then faces the group and tries to identify the missing person in one minute's time. If the Detective guesses correctly, he gets another turn at being the Detective. If he is stumped, the player who left the room gets to be the Detective. Players are allowed three consecutive turns as the Detective, so everyone gets a chance to solve the mystery!

To make detecting even more difficult for the poor Sherlock, from time to time no one should leave the room!

DOG AND CAT

and other word pairs

To play this game you will need a long list of word pairs that are commonly used together, and pencil and paper for each player.

One player is selected to be the Caller and is given the list to "call" from. As the Caller rapidly reads words from the list, the other players try to write the word that goes with it. The player with the longest list wins the game and becomes the Caller for the next game.

If this game is used over and over in a classroom or by a family, adding to a long list of word pairs will be half the fun. To avoid memorization, the Caller will want to be sure to read words randomly rather than going straight through the list.

Here are some word pairs to help you get started:

ham and eggs	soap and water
pins and needles	sugar and spice
knife and fork	strawberries and cream
salt and pepper	pots and pans
hugs and kisses	boys and girls
stop and go	comb and brush
shoes and socks	black and white
up and down	read and write
in and out	snow and ice
back and forth	right and wrong
thunder and lightning	hand and glove
coat and hat	fun and games
bread and butter	slim and trim

SOUND OFF
this game requires a good ear

For this game you will need a pencil and paper for each player, a collection of objects to make sounds, and lots of imagination. The objects should be hidden in a box or bag. Some possible sounds to create are the ringing of a bell, sharpening of a pencil, stamping of a foot, clapping, sneezing, coughing, a music box, or an alarm clock.

One player is chosen to be Noisemaker. The Noisemaker makes at least ten noises. The other players are not allowed to see the action and/or objects creating the noises. This can be accomplished by having players close their eyes or put their heads on their desks, or by having the Noisemaker turn her back to the group.

The object of the game is for players to listen carefully to the noises and identify them on their paper. The player with the longest, *correct* list wins the game and becomes the next Noisemaker. Keep an ear out for unusual sounds to confuse your fellow players.

I MET AN OLD LADY WITH AN "A"

use your imagination for funnier sentences

Players sit in a circle. The first player begins the game with the letter A.

"I met an old lady with an 'A.' Her name was *Alice* and she came from *Athens*. This old lady was *angry*. She was bringing an *apple* to *Andy*." The next player uses the letter B. "I met an old lady with a 'B.' Her name was *Betty* and she came from *Boston*. This old lady was *beautiful*. She was bringing *baked beans* to *Barry*." The next player uses C and the game continues through the alphabet. Each player must give the old lady's *name*, where she's *from*, a *descriptive word* and the *item* and *person* she brought it to, all beginning with the correct letter of the alphabet. If the player cannot think of a word within a specified time period, she is out of the game. As defeated players drop out, the game becomes even more exciting as participants in the play-offs attempt sentences built around X, Y, and Z.

A ROCKY GUESS-TIMATION
the closest guess wins!

For this game you will need a clean jar with a tightly fitting lid, small rocks from your backyard (you decide how many, just be sure your count is right), paper and a felt tip pen for the "guessing jar" label, and ribbon to tie the label on.

Count the rocks and fill the jar. You must make sure your count is correct. Then, make a label for the jar that says, "Guess how many rocks are in this jar!" Have several of your friends try to guess how many rocks are in the jar and record all the guesses on a sheet of paper. The person whose guess is the closest to the exact number of rocks in the jar is the winner.

Guesses:
1. ?
2. 478
3.

45

FINISH THE STORY
a round in creative storytelling

For this game you will need slips of paper with story ideas printed on them (mysterious happenings, tall tales, make-believe, science fiction, animal adventures, ghosts and goblins), and a basket or hat to hold the slips of paper.

Players sit in a circle on the floor. One of the group draws a story idea from the container and begins spinning the tale. At a very exciting point, the story passes on to the next player who must continue. The story winds on until each player has had a chance to add a part. The last player finishes the story in the most surprising way imaginable. Then another slip of paper is drawn and the next story begins.

TAP A TUNE

a chance to play your favorite song

This is a game that you can play just about anywhere. All you need is a head full of favorite songs and something to tap on.

One player taps out the melody of a popular tune and the other players must guess what song it is. The correct guesser gets to tap out the next song.

tap- tap
tap - tap

WHAT'S ON THE TRAY?

a simple memory test

For this game you will need a pencil and piece of paper for each player, a large tray or sturdy flat box top, a towel or other cloth covering, and a variety of small objects. In a classroom, items might include pencil, ruler, eraser, book, chalk, clock, notebook, stapler, paste, and paintbrush. At home, kitchen items or toys can be used. At a picnic table it would be fun to use natural items for this game such as a rock, stick, seed pod, shell, feather, or nut.

All the players except one leave the room while the remaining player selects 12 small items to place on the tray. The tray is then covered with the cloth and placed in the middle of the table. The other players are called back into the room and sit around the table. Once all the players are seated, the covering on the tray is removed for a short period, then replaced.

The object of the game is for players to list as many things as possible that were on the tray. The player with the longest, *correct* list wins the game and gets to prepare the next tray.

Variation
This game can become a listening game too by using the names of objects instead of actual items. The players must remember the names heard and list them on their paper. To increase the difficulty of this memory game, the player must list words in the correct order in which they were said. It is a good idea for the Caller to make a list of the words as they are given so there will be no problem in identifying the winner.

To add variety to this game numbers, colors, or shapes might be used instead of object names. Another time you might use names of people, animals, automobiles, states, or countries. On a day when you really need a lively game, nonsense words might be used to make this game extra fun.

OPPOSITES ATTRACT
an opportunity to think in reverse

One player is selected to be the Thinker, and silently chooses an object in the room to think about. The Thinker then gives directional hints as to the object's location. The fun of this game is that the hints must be given in exactly the opposite way as they normally would be given. For example, if the hint is "Look at the ceiling," what is really meant is "Look at the floor." If the direction is "Take two steps to the left," players should really take two steps to the right.

When the players have followed the directions correctly, the Thinker says, "wrong, wrong." When players do not follow the opposite directions, the Thinker says, "right, right." When the object is guessed, the Thinker says, "Opposites Attract!" The player who follows the directions correctly and first guesses the object, wins the game and becomes the next Thinker.

Some possible opposites to use:
backward - forward
light - dark
soft - hard
above - under
up - down
big - little

WHAT DID YOU SAY?
careful listening is the key

Players sit in a circle or row. (The more players—the more fun!) Someone begins by whispering a sentence in the next person's ear. This person whispers to the next person and so on around the circle or down the row. Finally, the last person says the sentence aloud. This usually provides lots of laughs because the sentence has changed in meaning so much.

A PENNY FOR YOUR THOUGHT

this game may make you rich

For this game you will need an ample supply of play money.

Players choose a category such as animals, toys, foods, places, or things.

One player (or team) thinks of a name within the chosen category and the second player (or team) must guess what it is. Four hints are given by the Thinker to the Guesser. Hint number one is a "quarter" hint, hint number two is a "dime" hint, hint number three is a "nickel" hint, and hint number four is a "penny" hint. (Hint number four should make the thought very easy to guess.)

If the thought is guessed after one hint is given, the Guesser receives 25 points. If it is guessed after two hints are given, the Guesser receives 10 points. If it takes three hints for a correct guess, the Guesser receives 5 points. If the Guesser requires all four hints for a correct guess, only one point can be added to the score.

The game can continue with different players taking turns as the Thinker until one side has earned 50 or 100 points.

Powerhouse thinkers may wish to choose more difficult categories such as states, countries, products, and professions.

WHAT'S THE GOOD WORD?

don't give it away

All players sit in a circle. One player is selected to be the Guesser and leaves the room. The other players then agree on a very special "good word." It may be a very ordinary word used quite often such as "I" or "you." The Guesser might have a difficult time noticing these words. Or, an unusual word may be selected by the group. Words like "hop" or "kangaroo" would require creative sentences from the players in order to stump the Guesser.

After the word is agreed upon, the Guesser is called back into the room. He must ask each player a question, and the player's answer must include the "good word." The player who gives away the "good word" becomes the next Guesser.

54

GOING TO GRANDMA'S
you'll be happy as can be if you make it to Z

Players sit around a table or in a circle on the floor. The first player says, "I'm going to Grandma's." The other players ask, "What are you taking to Grandma?" The first player then answers, "I'm taking an *apricot* (or any other item beginning with the letter A) to Grandma." The player to the left then says, "I'm going to Grandma's." The other players again ask, "What are you taking to Grandma?" This player then says, "I'm taking an *apricot* and a *baseball* (or some other item beginning with a B) to Grandma." The game continues with players taking turns, repeating the items already named and adding a new item beginning with the next letter of the alphabet. If a player leaves out any item already named or fails to think of an item beginning with the next letter, she is out of the game.

PEACE
and
QUIET

games to play alone or with friends

MY OWN IDEAS

SILENT COMMUNICATION
get that message off your mind

For this game you will need a few old magazines, scissors, paste, and some paper.

One player prepares a message by cutting out words and phrases from a magazine and pasting them on a sheet of paper. The second player reads the message and tries to answer it by pasting together a return message. Players may want to choose a specific topic to cover in their messages, or allot a time frame to prepare the messages. This is a silent game, so no talking is allowed! To illustrate your messages, cut out pictures and photographs as well as words and phrases.

HANDS ON
put your hands to work for fun!

Bet you didn't know how much fun you could have with your hands. Well, here are two hand games to help you get started having fun.

SEVEN UP

Players start this game by building a pile of hands. One player puts a hand palm down, and the other players add their hands one at a time to the pile. The hand on the bottom is withdrawn and added to the top of the pile. This is done seven times. Players then remove their hands one at a time until the last player's hand is reached. This player is asked to pick "yes" or "no." Once a choice is made, the other players ask three questions to which the answer must be the chosen word. The funnier the questions, the more fun it is! For example, if the answer is "yes," the question might be, "Don't you think your feet smell?"

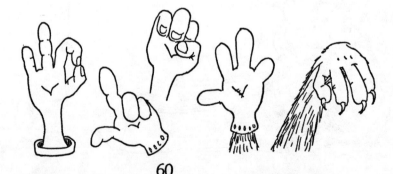

FIST FULL OF PEBBLES

Two players each have ten pebbles. One player secretly puts as many pebbles as desired in his fist and holds out his hand saying, "Fist Full of Pebbles." The second player says, "Handful," and the player with the pebbles asks, "How many?" The second player must guess how many pebbles are in his hand. If the guess is correct, the second player receives them all. If the guess is more, he must give the first player enough to make up the difference. If the guess is less, the second player receives the difference between his estimate and the actual number. The player with the most pebbles wins.

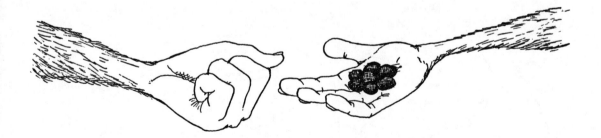

DON'T BE BORED
try these mind-stretchers instead

Copy your favorite brain teasers on index cards. Put the cards in a box and store it away for a time when you need something to do. Here are three to get you started.

HOW MANY

How many eights are there between one and 100? Answer - 20. Don't forget to count all the eights in the 80s (including 88).

HOW LONG

If six boys can pick six pails of peppers in six hours, how long will it take 12 boys to pick 12 pails of peppers? Answer—12 hours. It takes each boy one hour to pick a pail of peppers.

FIGURE IT OUT
10 LI - 10 Little Indians
7 WOTW - 7 Wonders Of the World
ACH9L - A Cat Has 9 Lives

DOING WHAT COMES NATURALLY

I SEE SOMETHING
do you see it too?

This is a good game for classrooms, parties, or families since it can be fun for people of all ages.

One person says, "I see something _____" (picks a color). Then the other players ask questions that can only be answered with a "yes" or "no" response. For example, "Is it big?" "Is it on me?" or "Is it alive?" The player to guess the object first, gets a turn to pick something he sees and the game continues.

DOING WHAT COMES NATURALLY
a pantomime game with a natural twist

For this game all you need is space to move around in and lots of imagination.

Each player selects a happening of nature—a cyclone, a snowfall, an unbearable heat wave—any natural event that may be dramatized with spirit. A player then pantomimes his selection in three mini-skits to the guesses of his fellow players.

An imaginative mime might depict rain by struggling with bulky galoshes, raising an imaginary umbrella in a gust of wind, and flipping lights on and off to simulate lightning. Another might silently become an apple tree and mimic planting a seed and growing into something tall, leaves falling, and picking apples.

The player who guesses the correct natural happening gets to pantomime his idea next.

SCRAMBLED MESSAGES

make up your own creative sentences

For this game you will need a pencil and paper for each player.

The person selected to be the Leader calls out a list of four to six letters of the alphabet. The players then write messages using each letter given by the Leader as the first letter of a word. Words in the messages must be written in the order in which the letters were given. For example, if the letters given are P, S, O, T, and R, some possible messages might be: "Please Shake Out The Rug," "Pete Slid Over The Railing," or "Pitch Some Other Time, Ricky."

Players then take turns reading their messages aloud. Once players become familiar with the game, the Leader may challenge them with more difficult letters such as X, Q, or even Z.

TRICKY TRIANGLES

close it, initial it, count it

This is a game for two players. For this game you will need paper and a pencil.

Cover the piece of paper with dots that form a triangle. Put one dot in the top row, two in the second row, three in the third row, four in the fourth row, and so on until you have a triangle the size you want.

The object of the game is to form as many triangles as possible by connecting two dots at a time either horizontally or diagonally to try to form a completed

triangle. If a player adds a line which makes a triangle, she initials it and has another turn until she is unable to form another triangle. The player who makes the most triangles wins. For added fun using the same paper switch to colored pencils and play a second game marking off larger triangles.

Variation
For a little different twist, play Amazing Dots. This is just like playing Tricky Triangles except players try to connect lines forming squares. When a player draws a line closing a square, she must then draw an extra line. No lines may be drawn diagonally.

AN UNUSUAL SCAVENGER HUNT
don't forget to look high and low

For this game you will need a margarine or cottage cheese container with lid, and a pencil and paper for each player.

Each person looks around the room and makes a list of things that are in plain view and can be found in the room. All the lists are folded and placed in the container. Someone shakes the container, and then each player draws a list.

On the signal "go," players move around the room to find the items on their list. Players do not pick the items up, but simply locate them and check them off their list. Players will need to be careful not to give away the location of the items as they are found, because many of the same items will be on more than one list.

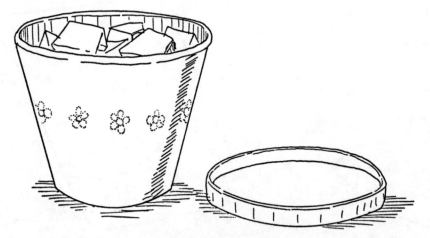

The first player to locate all the items on his list and return to his seat is the winner. He must then be able to prove his finds by going around the room and pointing out the items.

Variation
Each player makes up his own list of items each one beginning with a letter of the alphabet as he locates them in the room. The player who locates the most items wins. (Extra bonuses can be awarded if players can find objects beginning with harder letters like J, Q, X, or Z.)

WORD WIZARDRY

remember practice makes perfect

There are lots and lots of word games you can play that require nothing but a little imagination. You can play them anywhere—walking, traveling, waiting, or sitting. Try some of these, and then make up some of your own.

MAKE A NEW WORD

Find as many words as possible in a larger word in a specified time period. For starters try, "hippopotamus," "elevator," "alligator," or "wintergreen."

FORBIDDEN WORD

Players try not to use a certain word in a given time frame. Each time they do, they are penalized one point. The lowest score wins. For starters try, "me," "it," "I," "her," or "you."

YOU GUESS IT

Three categories are agreed upon such as sports figures, television stars, or singers. One player selects a category, says it aloud, and begins counting to five. The second player must name a person in that category within the time frame. If the player is unable to answer or answers incorrectly, the penalty is one point. The lowest score wins.

TITLES

One player picks a song, book, or story title. The second player must think of another title beginning with the last word of the previous title within a specified time period. For example, "Silent Night"—"Night Of the Iguana," or "Snow White"—"White Christmas."

INITIALLY MINE

Players try to make up a list of all the outdoor objects they can think of that begin with both their initials. The longest list wins. For example, if the initials are G.P., some words might be: grass, garbage, gypsies, and parks, pigeons, or planes.

SPELL OUT
find out how well you spell

For this game you will need to copy the game board shown, and prepare two sets of 20 cards each (40 cards in all) with words familiar to all players. Bottle caps, buttons, or small stones can be used as markers.

You can use the inside of a shoe box top or any stiff cardboard you may have on hand to make the game board. Use a black felt tip pen to mark sections comparable to the ones shown. The game may be played with two, three, or four players. On one set of cards, print correctly spelled words. On the other set, print the same words spelled incorrectly.

To play the game, someone shuffles the 40 cards and places them face down in the center of the game board. The markers are placed on "start." The first player draws a card and decides if the word is spelled correctly. If he decides that it is spelled correctly, he says "correct," and shows the card. If his decision is right, he moves ahead one space. If his answer is wrong, he does not move. If he decides that the word is spelled incorrectly, he says "incorrect," and spells the word as he thinks it should be spelled. If his decision is right, he moves ahead two spaces. If he spells it incorrectly, he does not move. The game continues until one player reaches "finish," and wins the game.

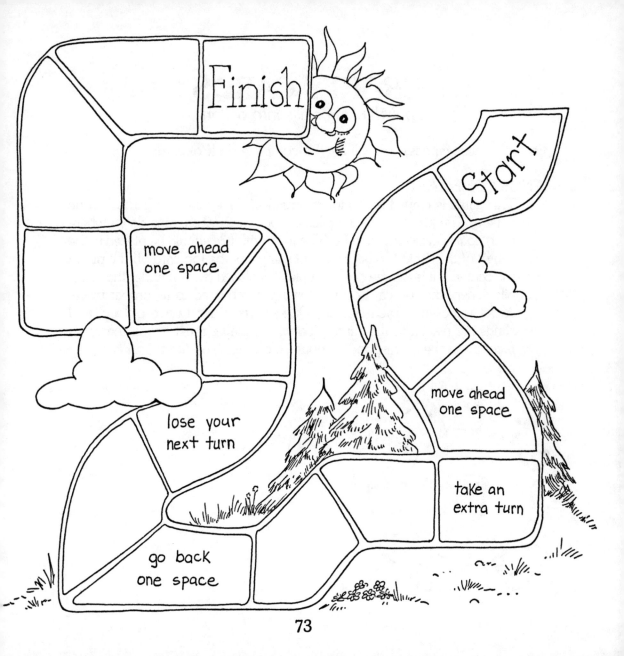

73

CRAFTY CARDS
put thinking skills into action

For both these games, you will need a complete deck of cards.

KINGS COME LAST

    This game is played on an imaginary clock face, and is a game for one person. The player deals 13 piles of four cards each, face down where each hour of a clock would be. The thirteenth pile should be placed in the center of the circle. To begin, the player picks the top card off the pile in the center. If it is a three, for example, it is placed face up under the three-pile. Then, the top card on the three-pile is moved to its proper place. Jacks represent eleven o'clock, Queens stand for twelve o'clock, and Kings are placed in the center. To win, a player must get all the cards face up on the corresponding hour before reaching the fourth King.

CONCENTRATE ON THAT CARD!

The cards are laid out face down in a random arrangement. Players take turns turning over two cards, one at a time. If the cards match numerically, the player removes them and puts them in a pile. If they do not match, the player must turn them over exactly where they were before, and the next player takes a turn. Players try to keep in mind where the cards are located and what their values are. The winner is the player with the most pairs.

LUCKY SEVEN

shake, rattle and roll

For this game you will need dice, and a piece of paper and pencil to keep score.

Each player in turn rolls the dice trying to throw numbers that add up to seven. Examples: two, five; three, four; six, one. Players decide on a number with seven in it such as 17, 77, 70, 107 to be the total, and the first player to reach that number is the winner.

Try your luck alone with this variation. Give yourself seven rolls of the dice to reach, as nearly as you can, a perfect score of eighty-four!

BUNNY BUILDERS

some funny bunnies are sure to appear

For this game you will need different sizes and shapes cut from construction paper (triangles, circles, squares, rectangles, half circles, or hexagons), paper, paste, and a box for the shapes.

Players sit around a table with the box of shapes in the center. As the box is passed around the table, players draw one shape at a time from the box. This continues until each player has six or eight shapes.

Players are given five minutes to paste the shapes together to "build a bunny." The group then decides which bunny looks most like a bunny and which bunny is merely funny.

INDEX